When The Dawn Breaks

A poetry collection about the first ray of
sunshine and the hope that comes with it

Pankti Pandya

/ BookLeaf
Publishing

India | USA | UK

Made with ❤ on the BookLeaf Publishing Platform

www.bookleafpub.in

www.bookleafpub.com

Dedication

To the thoughts that stayed with me in the quiet of the night.
And the hope that came with the waking hour.
To my parents, Shalini and Sapan Pandya.

Preface

Congratulations. You made it.
You survived the night that came with all of it's darkness.
If you're reading this, I hope you're beginning to see the
light at the end of the tunnel. It's not important- the
thoughts that plagued you, the regrets that choked you, the
nightmares that woke you, or the heartbreak that held you.
The important thing is - you're still here. In spite of all the
storms, you survived. In spite of the castles crumbling in
your mind. And you're only getting stronger.

This book is about drowning. But it is also about coming
up for air. It is about cyclones. But it is also about
swimming to the surface. It's about turmoil. But it's also
about growth. It's about coming apart. But it's also about
putting your pieces back together. It's about the hole in
your chest, in your room, in your life. But it's also about
everything that fills it. It's about losing yourself, and then
finding yourself anew.

This book is about the hours through the endless night
when you couldn't sleep. And the ray of hope that comes-
when the dawn breaks.

Acknowledgements

10:30. Books

I will bury myself in books
That take me to places other than the ones where I exist.
I will put myself into the shoes of every passing character,
So I can be them instead of me.
And I will go through this journey
From familiar beginnings to unexpected endings,
And stay with it through every plot twist,
Just to have some sense of permanence in my life.
And I will watch myself unfold, fall to pieces and un-become
Before I become who I'm meant to be.
I will survive on this air that seems to be growing thinner by the second,
And I will sense the disappearance of the characters that weren't meant to be,
As they quietly fade into descriptions of pages past.
And I will learn what to look for,
And what to value,
As I find it in myself.
That I'm made of resilience, if nothing else,
Hope, light and love, if nothing else.
And I'll find the right places to shower those,
With all I have to offer.

And I'll do it till my head falls into a slumber,
Switch realities and dreams alike,
Every moment of my life a passing story,
And every loss a lesson learned in parallel universe.
And I'll embrace all that life has to offer to me,
And accept it gracefully,
Come what may.
For I'm starting to believe,
That it does not offer you battles you don't have the
strength to fight,
And it does not offer you love you're not meant to hold.
So I will bury myself in books,
Way past midnight,
Because once the clock strikes twelve,
I begin.

11:00. The Act of Giving

I always thought my hands were meant to give.
To offer benevolence and warmth, in a harsh, cold world.
I thought my words were meant to bring light,
To chase away all shadows of doubt,
That linger in the furrows on your forehead.
I felt my voice was meant to calm.
My songs meant to hold.
My prose meant to say the things we're all afraid to
speak.
And so I unfolded, bodies of kindness,
Took the skeletons in your closet and hid them,
As if they were my own.
I celebrated as your friend,
Wagered war as your comrade.
I held your quiet uncertainty,
In the pit of my stomach.
I watered your seed endlessly,
From the vessel I was born with,
Never caring how much I poured.
For the world, I let my rivers run.
Because I believe, that I was sent to grow,
To touch, to heal, to hold.
Now the vessel seems to be running out,
There is only so much kindness that can conquer the

world.
There is only so much life left in my soul.
Only so much softness left in my palms,
Only so much love left in my heart.
But I still believe it's strong enough to change the world.
I still believe they're warm enough to shelter,
To protect, to provide, to preserver.
Sometimes there is strength in remaining soft,
In a world that's trying to wear you down.
And soft, I'll always be.
I'll always lower my voice,
Wear my smile,
Bow my head,
Make space.
Always hold your scars.
Always make you feel safe.
Not in submission.
Not in weakness.
But in kindness.
In faith.
In friendship.
And I'll still give,
All that I can.
In a world that needs so much.

11:30. Time

It's funny how the clock stopped ticking.
But time never stopped.
Except for the night we walked by the river,
And the streetlight reflected off of your face-
The darkness in your mind aglow
With but one candle in sight.
How the wind caressed my untucked hair,
And the truth stood between us,
Violently trying to force it's way in,
But you and I refused to address the elephant on the
road,
Instead bridging this space between us,
With all of our insecurities and all of our mistakes.
Dreams longed for and wasted,
Like faraway stars in the night sky.
Everything we were meant to do seemed decades away.
And yet time slipped through my fingers,
As it always does with a coy smile.
And yet the bridge fell to pieces,
What did we expect?
It was founded on lost hopes and broken hearts.
And neither of us took it upon ourselves to heal.
Funny, time should stop now,
When it has no business slowing down,

When all that remains here is an empty street by the flowing river,
The lights dimmer than they used to be.
The silence so loud, it reverberates through my soul.
Funny how people change,
Ambitions anew,
Dreams replaced.
I think I'm the furthest away from who I was
And who I set out to be.
But at least one of us deserves to be closer to finding themselves.
I hope this time, is all you need.
I don't think this will ever come as naturally to me,
As ink to my paper
And words to my soul.
All life wasted in effort,
Running away from who I am.
A fool's errand.
A vicious labyrinth.
A bottomless fall.
Where shall I find solace in it all?
My clock may have stopped.
But time turns over a new page.
And I can't seem to find my bearings today,
But come tomorrow, I hope I find a friend in the mirror.
And call it mine, just the same.

12:00. Ghosts

I walk a lonely path.
But I'm not alone.
My ghosts are regrets.
My ghosts are my secrets.
My demons sneer at me at night.
They reach out from the darkest corners of my mind,
And they rob me of my faith.
Till I'm just a question mark hanging in the air,
Like A rope that hangs from the ceiling.
And my nightmares are so loud,
They feel real.
I watch in horror,
As they shove hard pills down my throat.
Unable to move,
Unable to scream.
It's a punishment to have a conscious mind,
And dream such dreams with open eyes.
When I try to wake up, I fail.
Mornings are just a continuation of the nights,
But in the bustle of a singing kettle,
And chirping birds,
And car horns on busy roads,
They shrink in size until they're only pennies in my
pocket.

Only seeds strewn under my bed.
My muscles find their strength again,
And my mind finds itself occupied,
Until it's so overused,
That it falls back exhausted.
And these demons, they always prey on the weak.
They always lean on fragile shoulders,
Always tighten their grip around erratic heartbeats.
If I feed the fear, it grows.
So I close my eyes,
And I let it starve.
I think of all my favourite moments,
That were and are yet to be.
And I find the love that burns like a candle through the
darkness,
And I let it's warmth encompass me,
And cover me whole.
And the demons cower away,
At the break of dawn.
For there may be worse things,
But there are so many better ones for it.
And it's a matter of perception.
And fear may cower,
But love conquers.
And restores faith.
And anything that pure,
Always wins.

I walk a lonely path.
But I'm not alone.
My ghosts are my wishes.
My ghosts are my dreams.

12:30 . Night of Horrors

The night comes not without it's ghosts.
A prickling sensation begins at the ends of my toes,
Crawling it's way up the curves of my calves,
Setting my stomach ablaze.
A chill down my spine,
A tightness around my chest,
Hands on my neck-
A sickness in uproar,
A breath caught in my throat;

The night comes not without it's terrors,
Of voices past,
And painful surrenders.
A lullaby drowning into a labyrinth,
A desire diving into an abyss.
A pulse running wild and extremities cold.
A crowded head, with thoughts running wild.

The night comes not without it's tricks,
Of promises lost,
And hopes withered.
Of what was and could have been,
And what is and what else will be.
A moment lived over a hundred times,

And so many hushed into the shadows of mind.

The night comes not without strength,
To hold on despite, and survive.
For the matter is only as big as you make it.
For the headlights still guide,
And the stars still shine.

So maybe the night is only a monster of my own making.
And maybe the Sun no savior, only an escape.
But maybe if I give neither the power,
To quake my soul while it still shakes,
Maybe the night will come to me as a friend in grace.

And with that I welcome you with open arms,
Take me in stead, and lay me on my bed.

1:00 . Chasing Dreams

I have watched from afar,
Dreams dissipate into thin air.
The distance is always deceiving.
Somehow, I'm always a step short.
The distance is deceiving,
But so are the masks.
Worn on the sidelines,
Like they could ever know the stirring melodies inside
my soul,
Or the storms that refuse to quiet my mind.
The quakes that wake me from a failing slumber,
The dawn that promises light but brings only darkness.
For someone who likes to have a hold on things,
Life is constantly slipping like sand through my fingers.
Sometimes I entrust upon it, the ability to take me where
I belong,
But I no longer know if it is so much where I belong,
Or that I constantly try to,
Make a home in woods that weren't meant to encase this
fire.
And then this rollercoaster slowly sneers and turns into
a terrifying smile.
And I find that I'm no longer enjoying the ride,
All I'm trying to do is survive.

What was meant to be a finding of the soul,
Is now a constant spiral down an unknown labyrinth.
And I can no longer tell where it begins and ends,
I'm always at a turning,
And it's never possible to tell,
Whether the path is right or wrong.
Always the wiser in retrospect.
Now I only aim to not regret,
Nor repent on a gamble I chose to make,
Even if it means I set myself up to lose,
In the moment, it's always harder to choose.
I have watched from within an inch of the doorway,
The light of my dreams shadowed by desire,
The closer I get, the harder it is to reach.
Aghast, I see the doors slowly closing in,
I race and pant, and skip and jump across the stairway,
But the light is a ray now,
Seeping through a keyhole on a closed door.
I grasp the handle, and try to open it,
But what despair! Someone threw the keys away.
There is a thin line between the foolish and the brave,
And I walk it everyday,
With a vision I caught through the keyhole,
Finding those keys, my singular goal.
And I can't tell, which side I belong to.
Perhaps, only Time will tell.
Life is strange in different ways.

And it's hard not to be led astray.
But it consists of little details in the present ad the past,
And yet, to yearn for the "bigger picture".
But I'd still rather toss Time for the gamble,
Than let these dreams slip away.
And even if I lose,
At least I was willing to try again.

1:30. What if

I float.
In the realm of "could have been"s and "what if"s
Head in the clouds,
Feet on the ground.
I dream of impossible things,
But reality grips me everyday,
Tainting me in various hues
Of grief and despair, loss and longing
Of love and sorrow,
Of war and peace.

I exist,
Between fictions,
But in them too.
I shed my skin,
And clothe myself into the bodies I read about,
Building an alternative reality as I go.
I feel so out of place in my own,
That I search for a sense of belonging,
Hoping I'll find it in at least one of them.

I try to find my homes in the people I engage with,
The ones I've left at the threshold of my kitchen,
And the ones who lay their vulnerability in the palms of

my hands.
I'm not sure if they were meant to heal, or meant to write,
But I try to do both,
Listening to their stories and then telling them to the world,
Hoping I do justice to medicine and to literature.

I also look for myself,
Within the confines of my workplace,
Whether I belong more to the sheltered,
The burned and the wounded souls,
To the words I hold back,
And the lives I've saved and the ones I've lost-
Or to the words that smother me,
Until they're out on a page in a furious poetry.
The words that soothe me,
The legends that captivate me, engage me
And the stories that save me.

I look for the courage,
To become what I could not,
From the seven year old girl who dared to dream,
And the seventeen year old writing a memoir,
And I tell her not to give up.
Because it is better to try and fail,
Than it is to fail to try,

And let it haunt you for the rest of your life.

I exist,
In the pieces of the people I engage with,
The people that bring out different sides to my soul-
The people that bring out my best and my worst.
Their complexities build me and continue to.
I'm no longer the girl I was.

My soul remains a canvas in continuum,
As life paints me in different shades,
With experiences and people.

I carry many worlds within me.
As the world carries me too.

2:00. Melancholia

I've been writing songs about you.
It's 2 am and your name is still the song that plays on my lips.
I've been trying really hard to, forgive and forget all the sundowns I saw with you.
I've been writing stories about you.
About our first meeting- all nerves, all strange, all closed doors creaking a little late.
About our friendship, about our time, about putting our necks on the line.
I've been writing poems about you,
About the colours you painted me in,
The artful mess you created, a masterpiece you said.
The shades I could never have blossomed into, the hues I never saw coming-
And it all began with your eyes.
I've been clicking pictures of places that remind me of you,
How different would they be had you been?
Or had you never been?
Could this sunset be any dreamier?
Could it be any livelier?
Could it be a rising hope, a warm welcome into the great unknown?

Lately, I've been listening to music I'd have played for you,
Had there been music to define us,
To define this complexity, this whole wreckage,
This endearing damage that we created for ourselves.
This whole touching of fireflies,
This whole hanging onto burning wires,
To heat, to game, to play all we've ever known to gain.
Lately, I've been fighting a battle,
A raging war against myself.
Would there be a better tomorrow if there had been no yesterday?
Would there be a blissful present had you not come to stay?
So many questions unanswered,
So many words left to be said.
So here lies my creative expression,
Of a beautiful destruction, Of a loving mayhem.
Because it's 2 am and your name is still the song that trembles on my lips.

2:30. Playing Safe

When I was all of three,
I'd take small, risky steps
Up to the edge of the bed,
And teeter over the edge,
Not daring to take another one.
You can't fall if you don't dare.

My father taught me how to swim,
But he never pushed me over the edge of the pool,
He held my hands and guided me,
While my mother taught me to love the water,
Instead of fear it.
And I floated, safe in their arms,
On hot summer days,
Splashing about, I grew and learned,
Fonder still of the tide of the ocean.
But I never went into the sea alone, and never where I
couldn't feel the ground beneath my feet.
I would go till the water hugged my chest,
And that was as far as I'd go,
Even if I could only wonder about the miracles that lay
ahead.

When I was thirteen,

And we went to an amusement park,
I'd go nowhere without my parents.
But with them, I was invincible,
Nothing could break me.
Even when it got a little too high,
I wouldn't shut my eyes,
But squeeze their hand a little tighter,
And knew I was never alone.

When I fell in love for the first time,
I didn't know what it was,
Till I'd pushed it away,
Far enough away that things turned ugly.
Miscommunication built barriers,
Where friendship had once stood.
And I had only myself to blame,
For not recognizing it sooner.
But I thought,
You can't fall if you just watch from the edge.
So how did my faith break?

When I moved to a different town,
I was young and naive,
I was in the eye of the storm,
A world so together,
And yet so lonely,
When everyone was caged in homes,

And struggling to breathe,
And I'd collect all these moments,
I wanted to keep.

And when the responsibility increased,
I feared those who came before me,
Out of respect, I said,
Always a yes,
I didn't want to disappoint,
So I showed up, through every rain,
Every battle,
As I always had.
Do it hard. Do it broken.
I gave myself to these responsibilities.
And peered out of the window,
Into the pouring city.
So many safe havens shattered,
Lay around me.
A father caressing his daughter's forehead.
A daughter's hands joined in prayer.
A husband holding his wife's hand.
Another one asking where she went.

And I watched from the safety of my edge,
Because if you don't care, you don't fall.
And yet I felt these bones break.
My soul shiver,

Every time I tried to pump someone back to life,
And failed.
All these safety nets tearing off,
All these lives changed within seconds.
Because even if you don't dare, you could still fall.
Life could still push you into the deep end of the pool,
When you're still learning how to swim.
But the good thing is, you can always find your way
back to the surface.
Always find a way to get back up an carry on.
And everyone's had to, at some point.
And if you don't dare, how do you learn to jump?
And if you don't care, how do you love?
How do you dream?
How do you live?

3:00. Is it normal?

I feel this madness descend upon me,
In the prime of the night.
Is it normal
To wish I was in a different world
At 3 am at night?
Wish upon a different kind of existence
When I should be more grateful for this one.
But I feel like I'm in a constant lull
Pushed around, stepped on,
And strewn aside.
Like I'm losing myself in the crowd.
Blending into the walls I built,
And just what is this hole
That I keep trying to fill and fail,
Just what is meant to fulfill it
And just how am I meant to flourish in this life?
I wish I could love more.
More of the world I am in,
More of my surroundings
More of me.
But I also wish I could love less,
Of the things that have torn me apart
Of the dreams deemed impossible.
Less of the hands that have brushed across me.

And passed me over.

Less of the passengers.

More of the journey.

I wish I could drown myself in the abyss,

Of a cool blue sea

And find calm in it's torrid waves.

And wonder at the life that thrives still,

In it's deepest shades of grey.

I wish I could sit atop a mountain,

And draw constellations with my mind,

And hope it is finally far enough away.

I feel this urge ascend within me.

This urge to run astray,

Barefoot across fields,

Feel the grass tickle my toes.

Feel where my heart was again.

Instead of constantly living inside the mayhem in my mind.

Remember how to breathe again.

Is it normal

In the dawn of tomorrow,

To wish only for the simple little things?

For more of the outdoors.

More of the world, as it is.

So I can get to know it again.

3:30. Funerals In My Mind

Tonight I lay to rest
All the pain, all the worlds I hoped to conquer.
And watched them burn;
Ashes blowing in the wind.
Even Death was disappointed that night.
All these funerals in my mind.
In reality, I heard of no one and everyone,
All the agony in my mind,
And the rage in my heart
Because while everyone lost,
I was losing too.
I've been losing myself for so long,
I don't think I will ever find my way back.
Poetry flows from my pain,
Letters of longing,
And yet nobody to send them to.
Tonight I lay to rest,
All these versions of me I've been,
All these regrets
And these "what if"s like it'd have mattered.
Like anything matters at all.
Sometimes I'm convinced I was born in the wrong era,
Or maybe it's just the world grew up and forgot me.
And I can't shake off the feeling,

Like I'm not where I'm meant to be,

Like there is more to me if given the chance to express.

But my soul has been disciplined for so long,

That the box it sits in,

Feels more like a coffin, above ground.

Where it doesn't belong.

And I wonder who noticed,

Who watched quietly from the sidelines,

As I began dying a little from the inside,

And let it happen anyway.

And I wonder who saw it all, and said nothing,

Because perhaps things would have been exactly the same,

Even if I was set free?

Perhaps these cages are mental.

Perhaps unhappiness isn't the world's weight to carry,

But it's mine and mine alone.

Perhaps the only childhood I get is my own, and my child's,

And perhaps that will be for the better.

And everything up until that point is just a hold out.

Just a black and white world,

Waiting to be coloured.

Tonight I lay to rest,

These cyclones in my mind,

That belong to me,

But I do not belong to them.
And I refuse to be lowered any further.

4:00 . The Mortal Coil

Death has long since stopped fazing me.
It is a lot like watching the sunset.
I've watched life begin and end in a span of twenty four
hours.
I've watched eyes light up in enthusiasm and spirit of
youth,
And die a thousand deaths, over years prolonged with
medicine and madness.
I've heard dreams shared and conquered,
Delve into nightmares that cannot be forgotten.
I've seen legs dance beautifully to a rhythm,
And giving away, falling into dependence.
Often the bearer of bad news,
For those are the ones that linger longer,
That tremble the soul,
The falling apart into shambles,
The mess in the wake of absence.
The empty homes we go back to,
The silence of not-being is so loud,
It's all you can hear.
I've seen souls emerge and dissipate
Into bodies that are just that,
Hands calloused, mouths hanging open,
Organs that gave away.

Hearts that stopped beating.
Minds that turn towards a slow regression.
And I often wonder,
If the life a body inhabits,
Is the one given by us.
If a person really is a being of his own,
Or just parts of our soul?
For why does the emptiness remain in our hearts,
When they go?
This crinkling of eyebrows,
This memory of held hands,
And how you taught me poetry,
And told me of stories,
Long before I started writing them on my own?
This memory that you seem to forget often,
And remember less.
This constant dull aching, but you don't know where.
This knowing, that you're looking towards an end.
This slow perpetual state of going towards a final bow.
These wrinkles in your smile,
All this loss of fat.
This muscle, this bone,
This tenderness of your hands.
This groaning, this weakness,
That never seems to end.
It is this, I fear.
This feeling of helplessness.

This growing older and then younger again.
This inability to eat,
This exhaustion and wear.
For all you have given,
There is no burden, I swear.
Death has long stopped fazing me.
I stand at this lake,
Looking towards it's end.
It's like watching a sunset.
There may be darkness now,
But don't be afraid.
For I promise you,
Light will come again.

4:30. Silence

I carry so many silences within me.

The skeletons in my closet pile up.

The baggage I carry only seems to get heavier.

With words we forgot to say.

With rage that stopped short at the tip of my tongue.

With your secrets that you gave me for safekeeping.

I locked them here, and gave you the key when you walked away.

If there were ever melodies across this forest, they seem to disappear into the shadows.

There's always smoke rising in the air, but I don't see the fire.

I bury the seeds of the memories I grew fond of, but the land remains barren.

With the carcasses of our conversations- that died with the promises we made.

I give quiet funerals to our hopes every now and then.

I don't mean to sound solemn, only honest.

I only mean to say that heaps lie enclosed within the fog- that silence is like a mirage.

That there is only so much you see, as what I choose to show you.

But the deck remains within me.

I carry so many silences within me;

That the piles turn into mountains.

Only those who've traversed these woods seem to read in between the lines.

They can hear me through the silence, and tell the difference between-

The storms that have settled into a quiet sea,

And the typhoons that have been laid to stillness.

The rivers of unshed tears that have shaken my soul,

And the cracks and crevices of my determined spirit.

Sometimes, they weigh upon themselves,

Landslides, rising up my throat.

So I water other passions, find ways to cut roads around them.

The echoes of my lullabies, turning mute across the forest.

I find ways to get across, to destinations that may serve me.

To dreams that invite me, excite me.

To the enormous possibilities that live beyond these valleys.

To the future and beyond.

The silences don't suffocate me anymore.

They grow me.

As i grow them.

5:00. Grateful

Today, I thank the stars
For the abyss I was thrown into.
For the graveyard shifts that wearied my mind.
For the cutthroat competition that almost pushed me off the edge.
For the storms that I had to survive.
And for the typhoons I had to traverse.
I thank them,
Because as I edged my way through the gallows,
I realised, I wasn't in these trenches alone.
There were footprints of those that came before me.
And there were voices of those around me.
When I came up for air, I could see,
Those whose hearts had been torn the same way.
My travelling companions appeared as the fog lifted from my mind.
And I realised that the burden isn't mine to carry alone,
And that our faith in each other is capable of moving mountains,
As well as bringing life to those passed.
And that's why I thank the stars.
For those who made me stronger in my weakest moments,
And for those whose shoulders I could lean on when the

34

air got a little too heavy for me to carry alone.

And for those who let me shine up on that stage,

While they quietly carried my burdens.

And for the those that I could rely on, to swim me back to shore,

When my arms were tired.

So today, I thank the stars.

For my nights may bring darkness,

But they also bring me starlight

That guided me through this endless night.

And it's almost morning again.

5:30. Endings

And just when I was feeling like myself again,
Every fibre alive, with compassion,
Every thought entwined with empathy.
Just when I was starting to get the hang of it,
The fragility of life and balance the full weight
Of the responsibilities on my growing shoulders.
Just when I was reaching for the surface,
Feeling the gust of wind on my face,
I realise we're already at the end.
That the lessons most valuable,
Were the ones I learned from the mistakes I made.
Because while it is human to err,
It is also human to grieve.
I realise that the journey is more important than the
destination.
That the climb is harder, higher the peak
And that's what you're meant to be proud of.
That you show up, regardless,
Even on the days that exhaustion wears every bone.
Even on the days your mind is but a black hole.
Even on the days that your heart feels too heavy.
And on the days that you can't feel your soul.
And just as I was beginning to treasure it,
All these precious moments that kept me going.

All these people that made me smile on the days that it
felt impossible.
All this laughter I thought had died deep inside me,
I watch as we begin our lasts.
For life may part us in ways, like never before
But we'll always have what we shared
In these quiet corridors,
Among these soul crushing nights,
And we'll always own every moment that we kept
someone alive.
And just as it draws to a close,
I acknowledge that all things end,
So that new ones must begin.
But none of the goodbyes are any easier.
And just as the colours start to appear,
Into the black and white pages of our lives,
I realise that every good story,
That holds your hand and takes you somewhere,
Still has to end.
So that new buds can arise in it's place.
So that you're left with greater resilience,
Come what may.
And just as it ends,
I feel like I've found myself again.

6:00. When The Dawn Breaks

And when the dawn breaks
I'm feeling better than usual today.
All these precious people in my life,
Radiate happiness and infectious smiles.
You know, I've fallen a lot of times.
But I've always gotten back on my feet.
And you know, I always come back,
Stronger each time than last.
My heartbreaks only make me stronger.
My skin glows when I begin to look in the mirror again.
And I remember who I was,
And what I'm capable of.
Grateful for the world I've made for myself,
And for the one that built me.
And you know that's why you must remove the weeds,
Before they infest your mind, and eat up all your trees.
But I'm only returning to myself now.
Typing all my torture into tales.
I've seen far too much suffering, to suffer anymore.
And eased too many breaths, to forget how to breathe.
I've pumped too many hearts back into bodies,
To leave mine out on the street.
So I'm taking my voice back today.

And when the dawn breaks,
I'll feel like I'm myself again.

6:30. Come This Morning

And come this morning,
I'm learning how to live again.
Amongst these thick canopies,
And the scent of chlorophyll.
The noise of mayhem,
Watered down by the melody,
Of water drawing it's own course,
Beginning and ending upon itself,
Much like pieces of my soul.
When I close my eyes,
And look eagerly for the sound of crickets,
And perceive only sounds of birds chirping,
I find there's a world beyond our buildings,
And boundaries I've drawn around my mind.
In this silence and stillness,
And this pondering slowness,
Life blooms and it makes me wonder-
How different the world would be,
If we all followed our heart's desires?
If we all lived for the moment,
Before it's coming and far from gone?
And I think perhaps this is where love resides.
In the embrace of this gentle breeze,
It feels more like peace.

Like coming home.
Even as the rest of the world dwindles in chaos.
Like burying your head on safe shoulders.
And come this morning,
I'm learning how to breathe again.

7:00. Turning Over A Page

Turning over a new page today,
It seems I'm stronger than where I started.
I realise that the storms is where I find my strength,
Even as I reach home, drenching wet;
Shivering in the cold that the world bruised me with,
I emerge grateful for the warmth emanating beyond my
front door.
For the hands that carried me once, hold mine still.
For the arms that rocked me to sleep, engulf me still.
I read somewhere in a book you gave me,
That every choice in life is like a branch on a tree.
That one leads to another,
And they branch endlessly in different directions.
And anything I do, will lead me to a different place.
But the roots will remain, and grow deeper just the same.
And so I think I may not get to shield my tree from
lightning strikes,
And I may not be able to prevent the withering of leaves.
I may not get to seal my fate,
And carve out the future I want.
But perhaps there is strength in accepting,
That I get to choose my battles.
The ones I want to fight,
And the ones I want to walk away from.

That I get to grow, if not taller into the sky,
Then deeper into the soil.
That I get to write and re-write my story
Time and time again.
And that I get to decide how much space,
To give to whom.
I get to choose to bask in the Sun with all of it's glory,
And embrace the falling rain onto my cheeks,
And grieve the leaves that are wilting,
And soothe the places that my flowers have been plucked.
That none of it makes life any less beautiful.
That there is strength in resilience
And beauty in relentless hope.
That to persist in spite of the wipeout,
Is the most difficult thing in the world.
But I persist regardless.
Sundown after sundown.
Yet another revolution around the Sun.
Today we start anew.
With love.
With hope.
With faith.
With resilience.
With compassion.
With empathy.

With peace.
And most importantly, with kindness.

7:30 . Take Me To The Sea

Take me to the sea.
I want to feel the water on my skin again.
I want to gaze into it's endless expanse.
And feel the cold against my shoulder blades again.
I want to swim to the top for air,
And say hello to the skies again.

Take me to the mountains.
Life's gotten so loud lately.
I want to embrace it's silence again.
I want to marvel at their magnificience
So I can feel small again.

Take me to the rivers.
I want to listen to their songs again.
And find my faith there,
In their journey from the snow,
To the sea.
So I can feel like a part of a whole again.
So that I can find a sense of purpose again.
A sense of belonging, even as I carve my own path.

Take me to the library.
I want to drown myself in stories again.

Of great minds, and wild imagination,
Of the most life altering discoveries,
So I can go places with my mind,
And feel the air around me lift,
In creativity and curiosity.

Take me to the forest.
So I can revel in an existence beyond my own.
So I can talk to other beings,
And realise there are realities beyond our own.
So I can frolick around in the woods,
Lose myself in the scent of chlorophyll,
So I can feel alive again.

Take me far away.
From this concrete.
From this burning city.
From the loud.
To quieter places.
Intoxicating scents.
Take me as I am,
So I can begin again.

08:00 . By The Sea

When I stand by the sea,
And feel the salt air across my cheeks,
I can almost swear the water is enough,
To quench the thirst of my abraded heart.
And when I dive deep into waters unknown,
It's as if this is where I was meant to be all along.
So I swim deeper and deeper,
The tide cold and sharp against my skin,
Until the water runs in my veins.
It tells me of it's hidden secrets,
A world anew that I know nothing of,
And I feel life around me getting bigger again.
So even as I come up for air,
I feel like I've never breathed easier.
Like the chokehold of my city,
Has loosened it's grip around my edges.
And even though the Sun burns my skin,
I embrace the warmth it brings,
For I've never felt more alive,
Than I was around the heat of the fire.
And my heart leaps in joy as my mind wanders,
And I wonder if this is where I was meant to be.
In this realm of water and soil,
Where I'm the smallest I've ever been.

And you can tell your stories at mountaintops,
And wander about places you've never been,
But I'll leave my secrets at the sea.
Where there is always space for more.
And with each new curl of tide,
There is a chance to begin anew.
And I'll let it engulf me in it's waves,
So I can feel fulfilled again.
For when I stand by the sea,
It always feels a little easier to breathe.

8:30 . Home

I'm returning home today.
With the light back in my eyes.
A little colour on my face.
I'm coming home today.
To the things I call my own,
And the people I want to hold.
With rejuvenated spirit,
And a resurrected soul.
To the sound of my heartbeat.
And there's finally silence in my mind-
The noise replaced with only yearning,
For the familiar faces,
And musical laughter,
Of the people who make my home what it is.
Who make it one I long to return to.
And look forward to return to.
That no higher land or farther sea can replace the
feeling,
That I feel when I'm with them.
When I'm back here.
Today, I return home.
As sure as the Sun rises in the sky,
At the break of dawn,
After what seemed like an endless night.

With renewed hope,
And newer dreams;
I'll run feverishly,
To my comfort,
The nourishment of my soul.
Fulfilled.
And yet, with a higher sense of purpose.
Today, I return home.

9:00. Space

So today, I make space.
I wipe the dust off of my CD collections.
The music records, that once had to be played on long-forgotten devices.
I go through the scrawls on my old notebooks.
I acknowledge the knowledge I had, and accept the wisdom I didn't.
I collect the half used crayons and pack them in a box,
To pass onto a younger version of me,
That has yet to colour her pages.
I tune the strings of my guitar, and strum until I can feel the music in my soul again.
I clean the photo frames, as innocence stares back at me,
And I find the strength to start anew.
From a place of hope.
A head of dreams.
I read the stories I wrote,
Once upon a time ago,
Of fairy kingdoms and reigning queens.
Of princesses in towers,
And demons in closets,
With deafening screams.
And I wonder when my imagination grew smaller,
Closing in on itself, as reality seeped into my literature.

When it became quieter by the day, until it was barely a
whisper.
And now it is my only escape,
My only knight in the shining amour.
So today, I remove all of the things I don't need,
The textbooks that only served as a stepping stone.
The jeans that I outgrew.
But I also keep,
The tales I wrote when I was ten.
The drawings I drew, in the drawer by my bed.
The things that I created in my head.
And I think of all the goodbyes I've said.
And I evict the people who did not heed,
To my call for help, in my hour of need.
But I keep the ones that make life feel a little lighter
everyday,
The ones that water me, make it a little easier to breathe.
And I keep the front door of my home open,
For anyone who may need to quench their thirst,
For anyone who deserves to be a part of my world.
And today, I make space,
To become yet another version of me.
And for the people who can provide me with it too.
So today, I make space for nurturing our wounds.